Project Red Light

Project Red Light

Mark A. Bitner

iUniverse, Inc.
New York Lincoln Shanghai

Project Red Light

iUniverse books may be ordered through booksellers or by contacting:

iUniverse
2021 Pine Lake Road, Suite 100
Lincoln, NE 68512
www.iuniverse.com
1-800-Authors (1-800-288-4677)

ISBN: 0-595-33056-8

Printed in the United States of America

This book is dedicated to my children—Alyssa, Anthony and Marcel. I am so truly blessed by your existence. My spirit is uplifted whenever I think of you.

Love,
Daddy

Contents

Acknowledgements

First and foremost, I'd like to thank the members of my team who were the first practitioners of Project Red Light. They are: Ruby Grayson Sproles, Diane Egan, Jeanette Kasprzyk, Clarence Dennis, Robert Moore, and Arbrie Tynes.

This book would not have been possible without your commitment and efforts in making the program a success. After some of our early accomplishments I knew what we were doing was pretty special. I am extremely proud and fortunate to work with all of you and look forward to our continued journey to achieving excellence.

A special thanks to Lloyd Sineni for your leadership over the years. I wouldn't be able to offer others opportunities if it wasn't for the opportunities you offered me. I also am very thankful to the many others I've come in contact over the years who helped me to grow as a leader. The experiences are forever with me.

My family played a significant part in the process and I would like to express my sincere gratitude. I would like to thank my mother Cecilia Bitner for her love, belief and encouragement. The values you instilled in me especially the importance of teaching and developing others was so very important.

To my sister Linda Bitner who edited the manuscript. Thank you very much for your time, effort, input and support during the writing process.

To my brother Keith Bitner who inspired me to write the book. Your input and encouragement along the way was very much appreciated. It just goes to show the impact that a big brother still has on his little brother even at this age.

To my sister Yoani Hinton who provided thoughtful insight during the process. Thank you for your support.

To my lovely wife Lisette who was very supportive and patient with me during this whole process. Thank you so much for listening to me talk endlessly and helping me to reach my goal. You are truly an incredible woman.

Prologue

It is not the critic who counts; not the man who points out how the strong man stumbles, or where the doer of deeds could have done better. The credit belongs to the man who is actually in the arena, whose face is marred by dust and sweat and blood; who strives valiantly; who errs, and comes short again and again, because there is no effort without error and shortcoming; but who does actually strive to do the deeds; who knows the great enthusiasms, the great devotions; who spends himself in a worthy cause; who at the best knows in the end the triumph of high achievement, and who at the worst, if he fails, at least fails while daring greatly, so that his place shall never be with those cold and timid souls who know neither victory nor defeat.

Author: Theodore Roosevelt (1858–1919); address at the Sorbonne, Paris, France, April 23 1910.

This famous passage was given to me from a family friend right after my graduation from Marine Corps boot camp. I had successfully passed through a journey that a few are successful in achieving. A couple of years later, I would enter the battlefield arena and be tested well beyond anything I could imagine. We were victorious while doing greatly back then. The team's sacrifice, contribution and dedication truly made me a believer in the power and meaning of words.

Is there a correlation between Theodore Roosevelt's words from the past and being successful in today's business environment? I would say to being successful there are similarities such as mental discipline, perseverance and tactics that are essential to being successful. Those who are not afraid to take risks and use their creativity are relentless in achieving excellence. Individuals who posses the burning desire to be the best are not afraid to lead people through any challenge. These are the people Roosevelt referred to as the individuals "whose face is marred with dust, sweat and blood" and strive to do great things. Ultimately, only the strong survive.

The experiences in business to be quite honest don't compare literally to those experiences on a battlefield. There are no life or death consequences in business.

Though, there may be times where some may sometimes feel pressures that are close in proximity.

Within today's business environment progress on every level must be made continuously. This does not mean that teams must make the once in a lifetime type of improvement. Rather, teams need to make sound decisions consistently based on circumstances that confront them. Often these decisions must be made in a short period of time to keep up with ever changing business challenges and the customers they serve.

This book outlines an improvement program from start to finish. Most often you will read books that focus on a specific area like leadership, an improvement methodology, team building, or a strategy. This book differs from the rest because it contains all the above but connects them so the reader can easily implement improvement actions, weave them into his or her daily work environment, and see the positive results in a relative short period of time.

Welcome to Project Red Light.

Introduction

Why Read This Book?

The objective of this book is to provide leaders and their teams with a more lean and systematic approach to improve individual performance, business processes, and ultimately the service provided to the customer.

By incorporating Project Red Light into your daily work environment, you will lead employees to adopt a project-oriented mindset to work through challenges. Employees will develop new skills in improvement methods while gaining true ownership of results achieved. Most importantly, they will be given the opportunity to view processes completed daily from a different perspective. They will learn that a series of interconnected and dependent steps must be completed to reach a desired outcome.

As a "service provider" it is your responsibility to seek ways to improve all aspects of the operation to meet your organization's business objectives. Continuous improvement is a core component in business operations. And you as a leader must continuously demonstrate your worth to the organization. Your success today no longer matters tomorrow. The most challenging aspect to achieving business excellence is getting people on the same level so that a common vision and objectives can be understood, agreed to and accomplished collectively.

In order to achieve this level of success, business leaders have to make a concerted effort to make significant enhancements within the work environment and most importantly within themselves. Let's get started on outlining, step-by-step, the way to initiate Project Red Light in your team's daily lives.

The Red Light Philosophy

In daily life, we are confronted with a set of circumstances that are both expected and unexpected. We heavily influence expected circumstances in one way or another. People know the path taken and understand the potential outcome. When this natural phenomenon occurs individuals mentally map out their lives accordingly.

On the other hand we also can be confronted with unexpected circumstances. These sudden experiences can have both positive and negative implications. People most often will turn to instinct vs. evaluation when deciding what action to take.

This natural decision-making process is woven consistently into life's fabric when facing whatever situation. This repetitive cycle of experiences and decisions is the central core of what Project Red Light is about.

Project Red Light mentality is a daily analytical review of the criteria responsible for consistently meeting and exceeding customer satisfaction. The objective is to transition all negative experiences into positive ones. One set of circumstances leads to another set of circumstances and on and on. Variables affect the expected service delivery. It is every team member's responsibility to identify potential issues and understand how to improve service moving forward.

1

Team Meeting-Introducing the Concept

Due to the challenges faced with the economy over the last couple of years, companies have relied on and received more productivity from their existing workforce. Businesses have required more from their workforce by having them perform a multitude of responsibilities that a couple of years ago no one could have predicted. It is what is. A new dynamic business environment is evolving and in order for companies to remain competitive they are looking for their leaders to pave the way.

Leader's Notes-Commitment

As the leader, your level of influence is the most important characteristic you possess in making this transformation a success. Take a private moment to reflect on past experiences and think about how your level of influence has affected team performance and what your employees' perception might be regarding your leadership. Take an honest look at yourself and identify past instances where you didn't meet your responsibilities in leading the team or exhibited negative leadership behaviors that hindered high-team performance. In other words, recall those instances where you failed? Determine what is appropriate to share with your team that lends support for improving your team's future together.

For example, you could acknowledge that you are not aware of all variables that affect their daily work. Or have you recognized that a catalyst for achieving great things starts by increasing team member involvement in the improvement process. Some leaders that have built a trusting and respectful relationship with their employees will have little trouble maintaining a team's attention and receiving buy-in about the changes to the way the team works when proposed.

Some leaders will need to take a little more time convincing team members that change is warranted for growth on both sides of the spectrum. Be humble and sincere—it will go a long way. Employees are forever watching leaders. Leaders who attempt to mislead employees either by stating that a new sense of direction is always forthcoming without any action, or commit to changes that one can't deliver will find little success out of the gate.

Talk about "Purpose"

As the leader, it is critical that you state the reasons why introducing the Project Red Light Program will make a positive impact in the employee's life. Sure, any actions initiated must support the organization's overall objectives, but there are basic factors that will add value to any business. Employees must have a vested interest of some sort. What if employees could improve or develop business skills and simultaneously improve an entire process? This is rather unique but nevertheless an interesting concept worth exploring. The following are discussion points recommended for the introductory meeting.

- **Team contribution**—functioning in unison to complete daily work actions.

- **Self development**—continuous development of project improvement skills for long-term success.

- **Operational excellence**—creating efficiency in service delivery by eliminating waste or defective elements from internal processes.

Project Red Light Overview

Provide the team with an overview on how the Program works from beginning to end.

- Everyone will be assigned a functional role within the team.

- The functional roles are additional responsibilities above everyone's regular full-time job. The functional role requires a wider range of accountability associated to the work.

- Each team member is given a working document which contains "Service Success" factors that the team develops together.

- The factors will cover a wide range of service experiences that are critical to delivering quality service.

- Each team member will rate each factor based on daily service experiences using a basic color rating method:

  Green= positive experiences

  Yellow= potential concerns

  Red= negative experiences

- Team meets weekly and reviews each service success factor as well as significant issues or concerns (roundtable format). Each individual explains their experiences based on the rating given.

- Common issues discussed. Team brainstorms on immediate resolution (s).

- If team comes to a consensus on what action to take, it is implemented.

- If team requires more data to make a decision, then that issue is categorized as a "Red Light" issue.

- The employee overseeing that particular functional area (role) in which the issue resides is assigned the issue.

- The employee conducts an analysis and reports status back to team. The employee presents weekly updates on progress made. When the analysis is complete, the employee presents the final improvement recommendation to the team.

- Team discusses and votes on recommendation. If vote is split, then, leader will have the deciding vote.

- All meeting minutes, actions taken and improvement recommendations will be communicated to upper management and other groups identified.

- The functional lead monitors the improvement and provides the team with a progress report.

- Process repeats itself.

Leader's Notes-Functional Roles

Within a project team, members are selected based on their specific subject expertise.

After the leader presents a high overview of the program's concept, he or she lists the functional roles for employee review. The functional roles are based on primary services that make up the team's entire service delivery model. Functional roles can have multiple service categories or responsibilities that fall under one description. Functional roles must be connected to a customer in terms of its value or affect on the service experienced.

After a few days, get the team back together and assign roles. When you determine an employee's functional role, consider what their major asset is in their service contribution. Where do they fit in? Next step is to assign functional responsibilities that the employee will find interesting and offers developmental opportunities (look ahead). Mix it up. Most likely, you will assign roles that closely fit your employees. Although, it all depends on how well you know that employee.

One mandatory functional role assignment is the "communication" role. This role is responsible for capturing feedback in the weekly meeting and forwarding meeting results to the team, upper management and other individuals deemed appropriate.

Within a team, the functional lead has the empowerment to monitor and capture any issues or concerns. The issues or concerns brought to the forefront are the potential areas that the team could focus on for service improvement. Some team members may have initial concerns about being monitored by someone other than their immediate supervisor. If you take the time to carefully explain the potential benefits and guidelines to the team, then the team members will view this as just an "extra pair of eyes" monitoring the process so mistakes are averted or a specific action is completed. Therefore, communicating clearly defined roles upfront will be very helpful to setting expectations.

A key factor to a successful process is overall team contribution/effort. This factor should play a larger role in the overall individual's performance evaluation when Project Red Light is initiated since each individual's daily work involves a series of interconnected processes or handoffs. Leaders should communicate to employees that contribution to the overall team goals is the key performance evaluator. Project Red Light is a way of daily work life moving forward. Any individual who is part of any project team is assigned a role(s) due to their subject matter expertise and is evaluated on his or her contribution within that specific area.

However, the team's successes in meeting deadlines and objectives are an achievement of the collective unit involved.

2

Identifying High Negative Impact Services

Every service team delivers a multitude of services that occur behind the scenes and are transparent to a customer. These behind the scene details contribute to the success of the customer's experience. It is critical that the team understands the contributing factors involved.

Now that functional roles have been established within the team the next step for the manager is to ask the functional leads for service actions that could pose a "high negative impact" to customers. High negative impact areas can result if service delays and disruptions occur because actions are not completed within a designated timeframe.

Functional leads should provide the action steps performed for each high negative impact area. The team should meet after the list is completed and discuss each action and reach a consensus that the actions are in fact critical to quality in terms of customer satisfaction. The list will form a baseline on the team's primary areas of focus for monitoring compliance.

Below, are some examples of actual "high negative impacts" in a service support team responsible for providing customers with copy, fax and shipping services.

Copy/Fax

- Faxes delivered to recipient's desk within 15 minutes of receipt.

- Copier device is functional.

Outgoing Shipment Requests

- Shipment requests processed same day.

- Shipment delivery arrives on time.

- Shipment supplies readily available for customer.

Service Requests

- Immediate assistance available.

- Questions answered within guidelines.

- Professional and helpful.

Supplies

- Packaging materials such as box tape, envelopes and boxes are available.

3

The Red Light Worksheet

The Project Red Light worksheet can simply be defined as a working document for employees to evaluate and rate service performance on a daily basis. The worksheet will also serve as a journal for employees to document service experiences and appropriate actions taken to resolve immediate issues.

Employees will rate service experiences using a basic color rating system on circumstances that fall under specific service success factors.

- **Green = positive experiences**

- **Yellow = concerns**

- **Red = negative experiences**

Daily work experiences that are positive should be noted. A leader can use positive data in a variety of ways to increase service delivery effectiveness. Remember, the project red light philosophy is to turn all negative experiences into positive ones. Therefore, the team should comment on positive experiences as they occur. The positive feedback will rejuvenate the team's spirit and also acts as a confirmation to upper management that the program is achieving successful results.

There is a slight risk associated with the green rating though. For example, an employee may become complacent and rate service success factor (s) green to just get by the process. In this situation, you could hold employee accountable for negative work performance for lack of integrity, team contribution and non-compliance with a directive if an issue experienced by that particular employee surfaces and the employee marked a green rating incorrectly. The risk associated is negated since there is no positive gain that the employee receives.

Work experiences rated as "yellow" or "red" should include detailed information about the experience, immediate resolution if applicable and any customer comments attributed to the issue(s). There are specific sections contained in the form to allow easy entry of service issue details.

The employee can use whatever method they choose to record the specific service experience. The only stipulation that the team must follow is to submit the completed forms to the individual responsible for sending discussion points to the facilitator prior to the scheduled meeting. Providing the service experiences upfront allows the meeting to immediately start and allows the individual taking meeting notes to capture more insight into the topic raised. What is most important is that team members are prepared to discuss the relevant subject matter.

Here is a visual reference of what the Red Light Worksheet looks like when filled out:

Project Red Light Worksheet

Service Success Factors	Monday	Tuesday	Wednesday	Thursday	Friday	
1. Leadership Support	Y	G		R	G	
2. Service Delivery Results	G	R		R	G	
3. Team Performance	G	G		G	Y	

Rating System	G	Positive Experience	Y	Concerns	R	Negative Experience

Mission Statement: To deliver quality service on each and every occasion.

Employee's Name: Mark A. Bitner

1. Leadership Support Details

Experience #1: Mon.10/11: Manager forgot to schedule assistance in the dept. due to scheduled employee vacation. Meeting morning deadlines was a concern until I received assistance from the team.

Experience #2: Tue. 10/12: Manager apologized about the scheduling issue and purchased lunch for the entire team—praised everyone for their teaming effort.

Experience #3: Wed. 10/13: Out of the office.

Experience #4: Thu., 10/14: I requested an urgent approval from the supervisor in the a.m. to order a replacement part for a printer. The request was never answered. The printer malfunctioned in the p.m. and is still inoperable.

Experience #5: Fri. 10/15: No experiences to report.

2. Service Delivery Results Details

Experience #1: Mon 10/11: No experiences to report— everything went well.

Experience #2: Tue. 10/12: Customer complaint was received regarding an incoming fax. The fax was delivered 2 hours late.

Experience #3: Wed. 10/13: Out of the office.

Experience #4: Thu. 10/14: Received numerous customer complaints from Accounts Payable regarding the printer issue.

Experience #5: Fri. 10/15: All deadlines met. Marcel B. from HR complimented the service team on successfully processing the late shipments on Tuesday.

3. Team Performance Details

Experience #1: Mon. 10/11: Alyssa observed that I was experiencing some problems meeting a processing deadline and provided assistance.

Experience #2: Tue. 10/12: The team performed well— processed over 500 shipments within 2 hours

Experience #3: Wed. 10/13: Out of the office.

Experience #4: Thu., 10/14: All supply areas are well stocked.

Experience #5: Fri. 10/15: The entire team was assigned to sort mail. Anthony did not help the team in reaching our objective— he simply spent a majority of the time engaging in conversation with others.

4

Service Success Evaluation Factors

The objective behind establishing service success factors is to identify responsible service actions critical to meeting customer business needs. Simply, what is important to the customer's ability to function? Any factors chosen should have the ability to cover a wide range of service actions performed daily and variables that could potentially affect the employee's performance or service results.

Initially, you want to start with a relative small number of categories to rate. You want to get your employees familiar with using the form. Too many categories will impact daily work flow (remember employees still have a job to perform) or confuse them on the meaning of each (too much to remember).

Success factors can change. You can replace a success factor with a new one after the desired progress has been made to improve performance for that specific area. The leader should review success factors every quarter and identify if changes or additional success factors are warranted. In either case, it is important that you discuss with the team any potential revisions to the form prior to implementing any change. You always want to obtain the appropriate buy-in from them.

Here are some recommended success factors to begin your Red Light Worksheet.

- Leadership Support

- Service Delivery Results

- Team Performance

Factor Definitions

The factors outlined above seem generally positive and relevant to evaluating team performance, right? Defining success factors is an equally important step in the process. Employees could potentially define a factor differently if left up to make their own interpretation.

When I first developed the Project Red Light program, I listed potential factors that would be ideal to implement with my own team. I kept asking myself; what is important to a team's daily success? I listed many points, but one stood out more than the rest. A team's success relies heavily upon its leader.

If I am going to ask my team to be accountable for additional functional roles, and also ask them to identify and discuss issues that potentially relate to their coworker's performance, then it would only be appropriate for me as their leader to be a part of the continuous evaluation process.

Bottom-line, leaders are accountable for all team results. The direction and guidance offered to the team is a critical ingredient to reaching goals and objectives. At the same time, leaders will sometimes make errors in judgment along the way that impacts team performance. In order for the leader to increase their level of influence and effectiveness they must be willing to expose themselves to receiving upward feedback from the team.

When employees can provide immediate feedback, or question the leader's actions, it illustrates the leader's level of commitment to facilitate positive change within the team. A consistent green rating offered by your team can serve as positive reinforcement in how you lead.

Furthermore, a negative leadership experience can provide positive results as well. Leaders are not infallible. They understand that leading is an "art" and that there isn't one universal leadership approach that fits all situations. The art involved in leading is to remain committed to core leadership principles. However, leading also involves venturing out and using varying approaches to ensure that a strong team communication platform exists.

Defining the Success Factors

The following are examples of defined success factors:

Leadership Support

- Is the leader accessible, provide direction and guidance, schedules work, is flexible, and meets employees' needs?

Service Delivery Results

• Were the daily business processes monitored and results successful? No customer complaints, process or equipment challenges.

Team Performance

• Team is mobilized and performing to meet high impact service expectations.

Let's recap where we are currently. As described, the team rates success factors based on its individual experience (s). Key details are captured that are presented at the beginning of the Project Red Light meeting. Every leader has their own practice on how they conduct meetings. In a Project Red Light meeting, the number one facilitation responsibility is to make sure that the team is disciplined and maintains adherence to the following format.

• All team members are required to be on time and relevant service experiences noted in the Red Light Worksheet.

• As soon as the individual responsible for meeting minutes is ready the meeting immediately starts.

• The leader recaps the last week's issues and updates the team if the issue is still open or is closed. If still open, the leader or functional lead provides the team with a status update. If an issue is closed, the leader apprises the team of the decision or resolution.

• The leader announces the first service success factor. From left to right, each person is given a moment to describe the service experience(s). Each team member has a chance to respond with green, yellow, or red rating. The minute taker documents the experience.

• Team member feedback should be kept to a very minimum. Also, because some of the feedback may be relevant to another team member's functional area or work completed it is critical that you do not allow defensive rebuttal feedback to occur.

• There may be instances when the negative service experience requires further clarification and cross team member discussion is allowed. However, once the *issue* is identified then the meeting should immediately continue.

- The cycle continues for each success factor until all relevant experiences are captured. Your primary intention is to obtain as much positive or negative data that is relevant to assessing if a process improvement opportunity exists.

- Each issue identified is read aloud and the team as a whole provides input on how to resolve. There will be some process or performance issues that will be easily resolved. Examples include: a) minor change in a process step/hand-off, b) assistance from team members and c) communication.

- The leader determines the time allotted for team discussion. When the leader feels that the team has reached a consensus on the business objectives, the leader then recommends the course of action and immediately puts the recommendation up for a team decision.

Team discussion is one of the most important aspects in determining if Project Red Light offers tangible improvement in communication and the fundamentals of teaming. See, if members offer feedback (positive or negative) to make improvements then you know you are on the right track. Observe each member's reaction and interaction during the process, particularly how one handles criticism and positive feedback.

Remember, every member has his or her own individual qualities that set them apart from one another. As the leader, you will see how each individual further develops and grows. Acknowledge growth as it occurs giving feedback and recognition.

If the team reaches a consensus on a decision to a particular issue that poses no risk to the service or product, the solution should be implemented. Upper management looks to front-line leaders to make sound judgments on what is right for the business in terms of delivering service to the customer.

The leader's approved autonomy to make decisions should not be taken for granted and decisions should not be made recklessly. It is important that any potential change to a process is always communicated to upper management and the appropriate "approval" is secured. Surprising upper management usually does not end in favorable results.

- The functional lead is responsible for results of the change made. The team member will report back to the leader on immediate positive or negative changes observed. The improvement can be based on team productivity workflow experiences, service improvement results and customer feedback. The functional owner will then present updates accordingly at weekly Project Red Light meetings.

- When the team cannot come to a collective decision on an issue experienced due to lack of data, or more experienced feedback relevant to the subject is required then the negative experience or issue is classified as a "Red Light Assignment".

The last action stemming from a Red Light meeting is to summarize all service experiences discussed. This includes identifying and addressing issues with other key contacts or subject matter experts from other service areas that are part of the solution process. Identifying the approach to be addressed helps the team gain a better understanding of what the next steps are in resolving the issue.

I'm sure you can understand the importance of documenting every meeting's content and next steps for your own team. When the meeting minutes are complete, you should forward the meeting notes to other team leaders with whom your team experienced a yellow or red issue. These leaders may not be aware of the potential issues that lie within their areas of responsibility.

By bringing other team's issues to the forefront and communicating with them appropriately, you are assisting other leaders to potentially improve their team's performance as well.

5

Red Light Assignments

A Red Light assignment is an issue assigned to a functional lead. The identified issue is now a potential *improvement opportunity*. All Red Light assignments become projects and require in-depth review of the related process in order to develop improvement recommendation(s).

The next action in the process is for the leader and the team member to meet and have a strategy orientation session. The purpose of the meeting is for the leader to set the stage for the ensuing project by first reviewing the Project Red Light improvement fundamentals and establishing a collaborative working relationship with the team member.

6

Strategy Orientation Session

Get ready for what will be the most exhilarating and most intense part of the program-acting in the coaching role! All right, you have now put on your coach's cap, and its time to sit down with the employee and discuss the Red Light assignment. Both of you may have prior process improvement experience but you can't foresee exactly what the project outcome will ultimately be. If that were the case you both wouldn't be in this situation. Regardless, I can guarantee that it will be a positive growth experience for you both.

Coaching is essential in the Red Light process whether it is the employee's first time going through the improvement process or tenth time. Even though a systematic enhancement methodology is being followed, the project experience will always be different since issues have unique characteristics which may require a different resolution.

Those who act in the role of a Red Light coach must comprehend the importance of using various methods when instructing and training others on the fundamentals of a project improvement process. There is no set script which the coach must follow when teaching a strategy.

Another important aspect involved in the coaching process consists of establishing an equal and collaborative partnership based on honesty right from the start. As the leader, you will need to put aside some of the management formalities and authoritative behaviors that the employee is accustomed to experiencing. Your coaching approach will consist of your being an active participant in the process so the employee feels comfortable suggesting ideas, asking questions, sharing development and technical concerns and requesting further clarification on relevant topics or actions to be performed.

The leader should be upfront with the employee that he or she will be challenged and this is part of the learning process. You are a partner in the process, not a hand holder. Project improvement enables creativity, and as a good coach, empowering the employee to think through the necessary steps toward a solution is a valuable technique that will benefit everyone.

7

The Importance of Teaching;
Project Improvement
Fundamentals

Often, front-line personnel are given an objective that they either don't understand the reasoning behind or when working through a new process, they experience defects that limit the objective's intended goal. As a result, rework often occurs during the process to ensure that the service or the product delivered meets the needs of the customer. Negative elements such as complacency and low morale will eventually find their way into the team. These forces once introduced take a significant toll on a team's chemistry and productivity. The ultimate result has a negative impact on the efficiency or bottom line of an organization.

In order to compete in today's business world, it is critical that teams understand the basic fundamentals of how to improve the service they deliver. In order to be effective, a team cannot wait for an improvement program to offer enhancements to a specific area—let's say once a quarter. Furthermore, a company cannot rely only on its leaders to make change occur.

The simple fact is there isn't enough time in a work day to make this a reality. Leaders have taken on more responsibility and quite frankly need to rely more on their front-line personnel when it comes to contributing to positive change. Therefore, it is the leader's responsibility to teach his or her front-line personnel the fundamental steps to improve a process. Why? What better way to create real empowerment opportunities and get employees interested and vested into the business than by giving them the opportunity to provide tangible input into how the business evolves.

The team will gain the knowledge and skills required to identify potential root causes to issues and develop recommendations to enhance the service delivered. In essence, the leader has created a high performance team that can be leveraged to tackle numerous issues that may arise while at the same time maintaining the team's efficiency in meeting daily work expectations.

The project improvement methodology below simply is an alternate but succinct approach to improving process efficiency and elevating team performance in a relative short period of time. The next several chapters provide a general overview of the essential body of actions that when completed will increase the probability of a successful improvement implementation. There is a wealth of books, publications and software available on the market that offers more comprehensive information on each topic addressed. The reader can research to advance his or her skills later on.

Improvement Methodology Steps

1. Statement of Assignment

2. Capability Assessment

3. Create Work Plan

4. Gathering Data

5. Mapping out the Process

6. Analyze, Improve & Enhance the Experience

7. Control Measures

8. Present Recommendation

9. Deliver Change, Create Balance then Monitor

8

Creating a Statement of Assignment

If the Project Red Light assignment was already identified in the team meeting and discussed in great length in the strategy orientation then why is there a need to create a Statement of Assignment document? Simply, you need a record of the project assignment that can be easily referenced and understood.

A Statement of Assignment covers the following:

1. Introduction—provide background on the assignment

2. Scope—your intended deliverables

3. Workplan—schedule of tasks to be completed

Capability Assessment

To develop the project's scope you will need to complete a capability assessment. In a capability assessment, the goal is to develop theories as to what type of changes can be made to turn the negative issue into a positive one for either the team or the customer. The theories generated must be aligned with business objectives and intuitive for team performance.

Coach's Notes-Capability Assessment

Talk through the process at a very high level and focus on steps in the process where human error can potentially occur. If necessary, walk through the actual process with the individual to show points where issues could be initiated to ensure the lesson has been learned.

Creating a Workplan

The development of a work plan is an essential part of the strategy orientation because the intended life cycle of a Red Light Project is relatively short. Groups of tasks should be identified along with a draft outline at this time. It is imperative that a formal schedule of tasks is completed in order to meet the implementation date and manage available resources. The easiest way to organize the tasks of a plan is to break them down into various categories.

Sample Workplan Tasks

The following are sample categories for a workplan to implement a new mail operation.

- Data Collection

- Obtain Space

- Equipment

- Data Connectivity

- Phone Requirements

- Technology

- Labor

- Process and Procedures

1. The next step is to document subtasks which fall under each heading that must be completed.

2. Schedule a reasonable amount of time that will be required to complete those tasks.

3. Assign dates to each task.

You have now created a framework for the particular project. Remember, your goal is to develop a suitable improvement recommendation to the identified issue. Project timelines often change on a moment's notice. Ensure that you provide enough time in the plan for any unforeseen circumstances.

You should be not interested in taking on projects that could take months to complete. There are existing project management programs out on the market that will better serve more lengthy projects due to costs, dedicated resources and extensive progress reporting requirements. In Project Red Light, the interest lies in producing quick enhancements to the process. Time is of the essence in any service delivery model. Besides, Red Light assignments that are smaller in nature will be easier to manage and implement. The focus should be on calculated risk, speed and agility. The suggested timeframe to follow for a project's life cycle should not be more than forty-five days from start to finish.

The following is a "snap shot" of a workplan to create a new mail operation using the categories outlined above along with associated subtasks.

Implementation Steps	Duration	Estimate Completion Date
1.0 Data Collection		
a. Obtain historical shipping data and volumes on current business practices.		
b. Determine future supply chain needs and areas of importance.		
c. Complete gap analysis.		
2.0 Space/Equipment		
a. Measure space allocated for new mail center.		
b. Complete inventory of existing mail equipment to be relocated.		
c. Complete mail center layout design.		
d. Identify and order additional equipment required.		
3.0 Data/Phone Connectivity		
a. Build or activate data connection ports for access to network.		
b. Determine requirements for dedicated analog lines.		
c. Determine number of regular phone lines required.		
4.0 Labor		

Implementation Steps	Duration	Estimate Completion Date
a. Establish organization chart of Logistics Department.		
b. Determine labor resource requirements.		
c. Select outsource vendor.		
d. Complete role descriptions.		
e. Interview candidates.		
5.0 Process and Procedures		
a. Document accounting submission process.		
b. Document and map intended mail receiving, sort and delivery processes. Review and modify accordingly.		
c. Develop and document security practices.		
d. Create ship service request forms required.		
e. Establish service level agreement guidelines.		
f. Create reference guides for training employees.		

Coach's Notes-Workplan

Meet and provide the team member with an overview for creating a work plan, discuss work plan requirements and use personal experiences to support points of interests that you want to get across.

If the individual possesses high technical skills and has gained a full understanding of the requirements, then delegate the drafting of the plan to the individual. Allow just a couple days for the team member to complete the assignment while knowledge obtained is still fresh. Meet once again to review and discuss results accordingly.

If this is the employee's first time, partnering and creating a work plan together is an ideal approach to ensure that key knowledge is learned by the individual. Meet, review and edit the work plan together, and provide ongoing encouragement throughout the process. Track the growth experience over time with the employee, reinforcing what has been learned.

Gathering Data

After you have created the work plan, the next step is to collect data relevant to the identified issue. Here are some primary considerations while gathering data:

- Can the data help better understand the identified issue?

- Can the data help estimate productivity time spent to complete a process?

- Can the data determine the costs associated with delivering the service?

In every business function there are generally subject matter experts or SMEs who are most knowledgeable in a specific area. Most often, these individuals are at the mid and senior leadership level and often have significant experience on the job with the business function. They have experienced many issues over time while performing the function and have valuable feedback to contribute. SMEs are excellent resources and know other SMEs in the organization that can provide you the data you need.

In addition to SMEs, there are others down the chain of command that may not have the extensive knowledge on the subject matter, but have a broader base of the functional knowledge. These are often your front-line personnel engaged in the day-to-day grind ensuring that service delivery occurs. They may be very familiar about a specific transaction that is performed in the process.

Do not overlook the ability of the front-line personnel to provide tangible feedback on any given process step. They live and breathe these processes every-day and will most likely provide very candid feedback. Be prepared to capture all that is said because certain elements may play a role in developing a solution.

The internet is another valuable tool that offers many search engines to obtain insight relevant to the subject you are researching. If the internet is not readily available you can research relevant information at your local library. The information sought may sometimes be found in a business publication, a magazine or a book. You will increase your skills in this area only by continuous practice over time. You will need to keep a sharp eye so you scan a wealth of information and easily identify relevant data on a whim.

Quantity of Data

The question that most certainly will arise as you start to collect the data is how much historical data is required? The Red Light answer is: If you are examining time, errors or volume, you will need enough data statistics to identify trends and establish a baseline to compare potential changes that are made later during the improvement phase.

If metrics are already being maintained, and are readily available, then the optimal choice is to see a year's worth of data. It is not recommended that you use more than a year's worth of data due to the frequent rate of change that often occurs within operations such as employee turnover, streamlined operations or a change in business objectives.

If you are experienced in analyzing data then you could use minimum of a month's worth of data in order to establish a baseline average. As stated previously, each issue has its unique characteristics and the type and amount of historical data required will vary.

In summary, the key things to remember when collecting data is to use all your resources effectively (internal and external), seek out the data, ask the three key questions above, document, and gain enough statistical performance measurements to establish a baseline average.

9

Mapping the Process

Process maps are very useful to identify areas for improvement. Mapping out a process consists of documenting each step within a task or process in chronological order from start to finish. In between, there are a series of handoff steps that must be captured as well. It is crucial to show these particular hand-offs steps since there is higher risk for a breakdown between parties.

When a process map is laid out, all elements of a process is exposed. If a flaw exists within the process then it will ultimately be found under careful analysis. If the process map is complete, and accurately captures the steps involved, then you are that much closer to identifying the root cause and identifying a solution.

Some processes contain more complex processes with numerous handoff points, one right after another. In this instance, completing a process map will require a significant amount of time. Due to Project Red Light assignments having short deadlines there are alternative analysis tools that can be used to summarize large amounts of process information. One such tool is the use of a "cause and effect" diagram. Cause and effect diagrams can be used to summarize large amounts of process information into general categories to make the analysis easier.

The following is a "snap shot" of a process map design outlining steps for receiving and delivering incoming mail and next day shipment item(s).

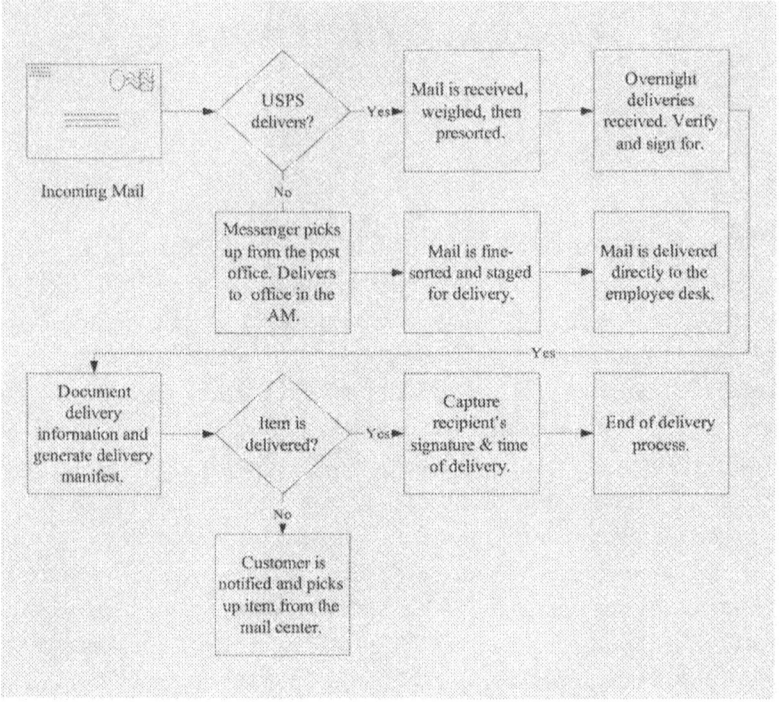

Exercise-Creating a Process Map

This exercise identifies different aspects of a single process. There are 5 steps that focus on identifying:

1. How overall cycle time can be reduced.

2. Steps that require a hand-off between parties.

3. Potential "break" points due to a manual or technical error/failure in the process.

4. Alternative steps that could result in same desired outcome.

5. Cost(s) that is associated within a process.

First, as the leader, you must identify team members to participate in the exercise and assign 1 of the 5 steps to each member. For each step, have the assignee fulfill the following request. A sample process map is available on the next page to compare against what is produced by your team, and assist you in guiding them along the way. You will see that almost all the process steps are highlighted in some way to help analyze the different areas for improvement opportunities.

1. Look for opportunities to reduce the overall cycle time of an existing process. This means eliminating steps from the process that add no tangible value or finding some efficiency in certain steps that will help reduce the overall cycle time. Use an identifier to distinguish. For this example, the pattern below is a "dotted" background.

2. Identify steps that contain a hand-off involved. A hand-off is an exchange between two processes. An example is when a technology action is followed by a manual action or vice versa. Whenever an exchange like this occurs there is the potential for a "gap" in execution time to exist. Use an identifier to distinguish. For this example, the pattern below is a "vertical line" background.

3. Identify steps that can be affected by human or technical error. Use an identifier to distinguish. For this example, the pattern below is a "diagonal" background.

4. Identify steps that an individual can potentially deviate from and still reach a favorable service result. Use an identifier to distinguish. For this example, the pattern below is a "solid shaded" background.

5. Identify steps that have costs associated. Use an identifier to distinguish. For this example, the pattern below is a "horizontal line" background.

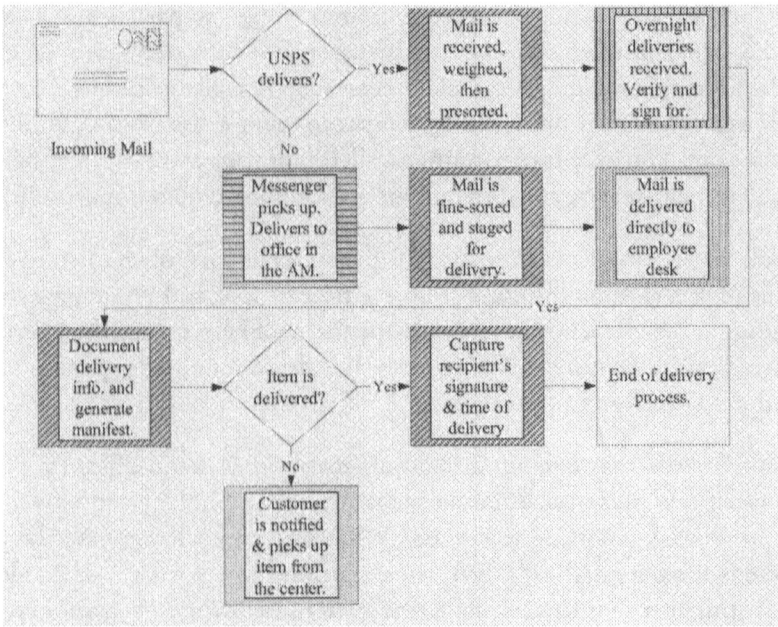

Coach's Notes-Process Mapping

At this stage, you can orientate your team on the fundamentals of analysis by providing a general overview of the techniques (e.g., identifying the 5 key components of the process) and tools (e.g., introduction to a process map). This purpose of the overview is to show how this exercise can lead to identifying process improvements. Discuss that this methodology will be used as they work on Project Red Light Assignments. The next step is to work on the initial steps in creating the map together so the individual starts off on the right track and feels comfortable completing the rest on his or her own.

After the individual completes the process map, meet again to review and discuss. Inform the individual to be prepared to walk through the key process steps and the approach used to gather the information. You should ask questions to determine how well the data presented supports the overall process that is being examined. The key is to emphasize how well the individual thought through the process steps to ensure the end-to-end process is fully documented.

10

Analyze, Improve & Enhance the Experience

After completing the step-by-step process map you are now ready to begin the analysis and improvement phase. I find this phase to be the most challenging portion of the Project Red Light Program.

The objective in this phase is to analyze both the statistical data and process map collectively, interpret the information and generate theories on potential improvement recommendations that will enhance the overall service experience. Teams sometimes make decisions that do not focus on positively impacting the financial aspect of the business or a customer's service experience. This occurs when the decision is based on the consensus of what the group feels rather than a tangible business objective and data to back up the recommendation.

The number one rule is to avoid developing improvements solely based on "subjective" feelings. People have a tendency to allow personal experience or opinions to be the sole driver for the action taken. Keep focus on the objective of the Project Red Light assignment. Always enhance the service experience. This means analyzing the process and its interdependent steps that involve employee performance delivering the service; identifying the overall business benefit to the company; and delivering quality customer service.

The improvement is a vehicle or means to gain a level of satisfaction. Conducting thorough research will prepare you to uncover improvement opportunities for a win-win situation.

Now that your team has gathered some initial data related to the issue, it is time to begin interpreting the data and evaluating the next course of action.

Benefits of Interpreting Data

- Identifying data trends can formulate problem areas and possible alternative solutions.

- Data trends can offer insight in determining where employee productivity is high or needs improvement related to total number of volume outputs achieved.

- Experiments can be conducted by deleting, adjusting or adding controlled variables to the process and then measuring the impact from the adjustments made.

- Metrics gathered can be used as basis for making work and volume output improvements.

Employee Productivity

Here are some fundamental steps to determine employee productivity:

1. Data provides the evaluator with valid statistics on wide ranges of elements including work performance. If a timeframe can be associated to a specific work function, then a baseline can be calculated to assess resource requirements.

2. Once time is associated with a work function or task, then a timeline of events can be plotted. To create a timeline:

3. Draw a horizontal line (on paper or using a software application).

4. On the left side, indicate the scheduled start time

5. On the right side, or end of the line, indicate the scheduled end time.

6. Using vertical lines to break out the work day into hours. For each hour, indicate the tasks performed.

7. Once the timeline is complete, identify gaps in time that can be used to introduce increased employee productivity.

Here is a sample timeline outlining work tasks for a mail operation.

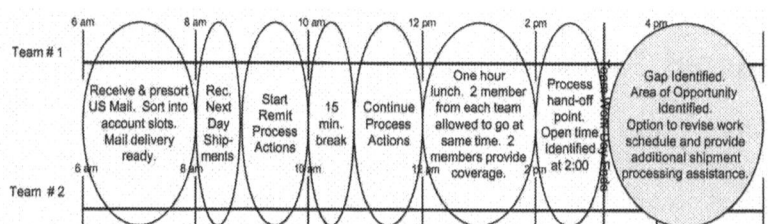

Process Map Analysis

The objective is to review each step in the process and identify points in the process that offers the opportunity for positive change to occur. Develop theories on what problematic issues are present or what enhancements might be accomplished. Start to visualize what positive impact will occur if the enhancement is introduced. There may also be some initial changes that are not necessarily perceived as positive in the short-term (e.g., learning curve, different process, etc.). Reading a process map is like reading a story. There is an introduction where the process starts, followed by the main content, and concludes with an ending.

You are empowering your team to implement changes to processes after it is proven that the change will bring positive results. Part of the enhancement process is to ensure standards are established for the process to ensure the utmost efficiency. Consistency in procedures increases the probability that the same outputs are achieved. This consistency increases the probability that service delivery is performed according to predefined agreements which leads to higher customer satisfaction.

As the leader, communicate the established service delivery agreement. Make your team partners in the process by reviewing, providing input and committing to the service levels defined for the customer. Always remember that the customer only cares about the service received. They are indifferent as to how the result is achieved.

For this reason, testing the recommended solution is critical prior to implementation. Pilot the solution in a controlled environment and include key members from all impacted areas. Identifying the potential risks that come with the new solution is part of the selection process. Consider the impact of any potential risk that may result from the change. Can you identify ways to avoid the possible risks or minimize the impact? These variables should also be integrated in the overall solution.

Calculated Risks

Those who aspire to achieve great things do so by taking risks at some point during their career. Now, the argument could be that some of those individuals regardless of occupation were lucky and their road to success could have taken a different route at any point. Sure. An element of good fortune does play some very limited part. However, do not be misled. A person will be confronted at some point to take risks in order to achieve the level of success desired. There is no way around it.

So, what advice could be given on taking risks? The first thing you should know is that there are two types of risks: 1) risks or 2) calculated risks. Within Project Red Light, you are interested in taking only those risks that are calculated.

A calculated risk is an action taken based on statistical probability estimates on what certain variables will have on the process. The careful measures taken mitigate the element of surprise that is associated with plain risk.

Real Time Analysis; Observing the Process

Another analysis technique is to observe the entire process as it is being executed. There is a high probability that improvement opportunities will be identified by viewing the process in real time. A process map does not provide insight into key behavioral factors when steps are being acted out. You have to keep an open mind during the analysis and be prepared to observe the process from a different perspective.

Let's say you have completed an analysis on a process and have made some quantifiable improvements to it only to later experience similar issues before the process was changed. The reason might be that the processes from its initial steps are somewhat defective to begin with. As humans, our mindset is programmed to view processes in basic or general ways from its beginning, then its middle components and then the final outcome. It is very important to map out the process from beginning to end to fully understand the internal functional steps involved.

There may be instances where observing the process hands-on is necessary to identifying improvement opportunities. To illustrate the point, I decided on a process that most people would be most familiar with such as: the preparation and consumption of a banana. I believe it quite remarkably shows the significance of what observation can contribute to an analysis. In order to gain a full understanding I am going to ask that some visualization on your part be used.

First ask yourself how does a human usually prepare to eat a banana? Most individuals take hold of a banana (with stem at the top) then pull on the stem and peel the skin layers until the banana is exposed. Then, the individual starts to consume the banana. That was a pretty simple process that achieved the desired result. However, sometimes the desired result is not always the most efficient.

Now, let's observe how a monkey prepares to eat a banana? A monkey will grab a banana from a tree with the stem up because in all probability it is hanging from a tree. However, monkeys then hold the banana by the stem and pinch the high soft end. By pinching the soft end, the action gently forces open the banana and remarkably the skin separates into different sections for easy peeling. Monkeys then follow the same process as humans—peel the skin layers and start to consume the banana.

The analysis diagnosis might conclude that the monkey's process of eating a banana is an easier, faster and cleaner method to peeling the banana skin layers than the usual practice by all of us. Our process is sometimes slowed down by the struggle with the stem which sometimes requires a knife or results in a mushy banana. Both processes differ though the same result was achieved. From a data perspective, you still have to lean towards the monkey's preferred method since a monkey existed well before mankind. C'mon, you have to love that one.

The main objective for providing this example is not to change the way you peel a banana but to support the theory that a process should always be looked at in different ways to see if there is an alternate way to accomplish the same task. We sometimes rely too much on what has been passed along to be the absolute truth and not be questioned.

In summary, you should be able to identify areas during the analysis phase that have a high improvement probability associated. The improvement theories being formed should be driven by supporting data.

Analysis Summary

The key components to conducting analysis are to; gather data, map the process, minimize subjective feelings, use the data to generate improvement ideas, develop baseline metrics to measure progress, conduct thorough testing, and keep focused on the overall issue which ultimately translates to improving service delivery and overall customer service.

11

Testing and Situational Positioning

The next step is to validate or eliminate theories by putting the improvement ideas to the test. As a reminder, the ultimate goal is to improve the service experience for the:

- Employee (performance)

- Business (efficiency)

- Customer (satisfaction)

As you test changes to the process, you will gain important information on how to improve the service experience for the employee and most importantly the customer. It is critical that both positive and negative consequences for each experimental change are captured.

The objective is to determine the best probability for success. In other words—what changes offer the best chance to obtain a long-standing improvement that will be easily manageable and sustainable over time? By categorizing the pros and cons of each improvement idea or process change you will be better able to strategically position the idea for gaining the executive approval for implementing the change.

The testing process includes situational idea positioning. Situational idea positioning takes into consideration the potential reaction of management who ultimately decides whether to implement the recommended solution. If an improvement recommendation has significant benefits associated, but perceived by some as too great of a change, or requires a complex change management process, then management will be very cautious to move forward on the action so quickly.

Most likely, management will almost always request further information and time to evaluate and consider the recommendation. Plan ahead. When first developing your plan, be as thorough as possible and think the project through to avoid not having a complete package for management to consider. Remember that projects usually lose their momentum as they are prolonged. The impact of the proposed process improvement and its related benefit vs. the learning curve to achieve the benefit must be considered. Sometimes less benefits and a shorter learning curve may be the best recommendation. The need for positioning your idea in the best possible way prior to making the recommendation is critical.

Your priority is to get the improvement recommendation approved the first time around. Make the necessary concessions to your intended audience while you are still in the planning phase vs. having to go back after-the-fact. You may feel that such a move seems political which may be somewhat disconcerting but it is a necessary part of the process. Rather than be consumed with the amount of thoroughness and detail associated, look at it from a positive perspective.

Coach's Notes-Testing & Situational Positioning

You will need to be a bouncing board for your employees' ideas. Be firm and require clarity when ideas are vague. However, show tremendous support and enthusiasm when ideas are right on track. Your objective is to have the team member think through all the data and keep them on track to reaching the business objective.

At times, remind the presenter who he or she will be selling the idea to. What is the makeup of the decision-making audience? Then, list those individuals that are part of the decision making process (team members, executives, etc.). Discuss each person listed, their leadership characteristics and any past interactions that exposed what factors they generally consider when making decisions.

Use what I call the "Question Gauntlet" method to assist in the process. Ask a series of questions that will help ascertain what reactions you can prepare for. Some questions to ask:

- Will he or she support this? Why not?

- Is the individual analytical and want details before making a decision?

- Is the individual focused more on customer service and tend to go along with an idea because of the benefits associated for the customer?

- Is the individual conservative in nature, set in his or her own ways and is not open to change?

- Does the individual look at cost factors as a major influence in making change decisions?

- Does the individual favor process changes that are intuitive and easily understood in making decisions?

- Does the individual tend to make decisions based on what the consensus of the group is (e.g., along party lines)?

- Does the individual tend to be negative and critical to any change recommended? If so, then the individual is embedded in their old ways of running operations and might view your idea as a challenge to the status quo of operating. Such individuals will attempt to derail the plan if given the opportunity or at least prolong the decision making process.

- Is the individual a quick decision maker or tend to be evasive or slow to react and require constant follow-up or pursuing to obtain his or her decision?

Make educated assumptions to project the reactions of the decision-making body. Review your ideas and tweak accordingly so that the ideas have the highest probability of being supported and more likely approved at the time the initial recommendation is made. You will not please everyone.

However, you should take into consideration individual reactions in order to move your recommendation from the idea stage to the "let's go" implementation stage. If the team member generates an idea that seems "out of the box," make sure you do not disregard what is said. Document all ideas. When an individual uses creative thinking it often times leads to solid solutions. It isn't the initial idea that turns into solid improvement solutions, but rather it is the spark of new ideas which often lead to the overall success realized. You will run through the idea several times until the final product is finished.

Sometimes, the final product varies greatly from the initial vision but it is the initial vision that got you there. So, always be supportive of creative thinking at all times.

12

Control Plan

After implementing the process change, monitoring the results is necessary to ensure that a positive result is consistently achieved. To measure progress, you should keep it as simple as possible. The main denominator to measure should be directly linked to the corresponding issue and benefit first identified.

The second measurable to track is to obtain employee feedback relating to how well the new process can be executed—how intuitive is it? The third is team compliance following the new process steps. The new process will only be as successful if those practices are followed and enforced. All improvements should be flexible in nature and constantly reviewed for additional enhancement opportunities. The skills required in knowing when a process has become stagnant are not born overnight. A team strategy must be born so process results are monitored on a continuous basis.

As all team members become knowledgeable on the Project Red Light improvement methods and fundamentals a "See and Respond" strategy can be introduced to monitor improvements implemented and other work completed as a whole. The See and Respond strategy involves all team members looking at variables that can pose a risk to delivering quality service on each and every occasion. All team members are given the autonomy to act on negative process variables seen at any given moment to ensure that the service outcome produced is a favorable one.

In a normal business environment the only individuals given this type of responsibility are usually leads, supervisors and managers. The problem with this is that no one person can be around every action at all times. The more you can train your front-end personnel to become more knowledgeable about how processes work internally, they will be able to see potential issues before they occur and inclined to either make the necessary service adjustments themselves.

In turn, their confidence level naturally increases and they become more interested in the results of their work effort. They will transition from a "task" oriented mind-set to a "project" oriented mind-set that is based on achieving value add to the company. During their progression they will see that their actions or ideas are truly appreciated and will develop a vested interest in the business in which they serve.

13

Presenting the Recommendation

You have reached the final stage and are ready to develop your recommendation into a formal presentation. Creating an Executive Summary Document and slide presentation is the final requirement. The executive summary is a one-page document that contains a brief description outlining the issue and objective of the Red Light assignment. The body of the document will contain bullet points that address analysis points and support the appropriate recommendation.

Executive Summary Document

The following outline can be used to create the Executive Summary Document.

Project Introduction

• Provide background on current situation or issue.

State Vision

• State the goal of the Red Light Assignment (e.g., To improve…).

Analysis Results-Supporting the Vision

• Bullet point benefits/challenges

• Process

• Customer

• Cost

Recommendation

Identify the improvement that will resolve the issue and enhance the experience. The slide presentation will contain some of the similar information contained in the Executive Summary Document. The main difference between the two is that the slide presentation is used to share your recommendation with the team. The Executive Summary Document is for management review only.

The team member is responsible for creating the presentation from scratch. Encourage the individual to pick a theme that best represents the recommendation to include; selecting a graphics background, a color scheme, layout design and word format. Ensure that the activity is fun and motivational to the team member. He or she has come a long way in the improvement journey so allow them to add their personal touch to the finished product.

Here lies an opportunity for the employee to learn or further develop his or her skills in developing a presentation. Individuals will increase their written and technical skills when completing both actions.

Giving a presentation in front of an audience for the first time can trigger some anxiety. Have the member practice the presentation in front of you as many times necessary until you are both confident that the recommendation is ready to be presented.

Attempt to keep the presentation timeframe somewhat brief with enough time for audience members to ask questions. This exercise is intended to increase the individual's confidence to communicate to others and improve overall presentation skills.

14

Esprit de Corps; Contribution, Welfare for One Another, Honor

Have you ever considered what makes a team truly successful? What probably comes to mind are such attributes as communication, collaboration, goal setting and leadership?

Sure. These are important factors but what brings individuals close together to consistently reach their objectives is a sense of Esprit de Corps. Having served in the United States Marine Corps, I experienced first-hand the value and positive impact when a team experiences Esprit de Corps. It is not the word itself that makes the difference but rather its meaning.

In my opinion, Esprit de Corps means a shared inspirational spirit and bond that develops within a team when members exhibit respect and loyalty to each other and a deep commitment to team principles. This is a very important component and the team can achieve significant results beyond standard boundaries once it is established.

The three core factors critical to establishing a common spirit among teams members are:

- **Contribution**—to play a significant role in a result achieved.

- **Welfare for One Another**—aid those in needs.

- **Honor**—the respect, integrity and sense of pride one feels and shows in response to being a part of something that is bigger than one's self.

Contribution

Each individual, regardless of his or her role must clearly **understand** what is required in terms of performance in that role, why he or she is a **perfect fit** for that role, and what **value** they will contribute to reach the objective.

A general job description lists requirements expected within that position, right? All team members are expected to meet or exceed the performance criteria established. The leader uses these guidelines as a baseline to measure job performance. Often what happens is that there are certain individuals who excel while others have specific skill sets that allow them to perform at a high level in a certain functional area while other areas require further development.

The high performers always receive the most praise and understandably are trusted and often times obtain special types of assignments. Other team members while still important to a team's functionality, experience less praise and receive less special assignments. This approach seems reasonable in nature and can be easily justified under many circumstances.

There is a slight problem when such a management style is used. If a leader follows this approach they will creating an internal conflict that will manifest within the team, and at some point, will be counterproductive to the team's productivity. How could this be? How could a special assignment to a high performer have negative consequences? The leader is unintentionally creating an atmosphere of negative consequences. In other words, you are saying the winner will always be the one with the ability to get to the finish line first? Those high performers will always have an advantage over others regardless if they increased their level of performance simply due to the perception that has been established.

In a team, *all roles are important.* Help your team realize their potential. When those special assignments or projects arise it is your responsibility as a leader to equally assign those types of challenges each team member. The experience alone will offer the individual tremendous growth and development.

Welfare for One Another

Welfare for one another simply means naturally assisting another team member in need. A leader cannot literally make an individual care for someone else. A leader can only foster an environment that continuously promotes relationship growth and teaming.

People spend a majority of their life being in the workplace. The leader should establish a work environment that is safe, enjoyable, interesting and contains a tangible support network within the team. Ensuring that individuals are cross-trained on all functions is very important so employees do not feel a level of anxiety when called upon to fill a role temporarily.

Another element not often talked about is personal variables that can affect an employee's work performance on any given day. Certain personal events such as feeling under the weather, child-care issues, or caring for a family member who is ill, all have the potential to impact work performance based on the employee's lack of mental focus. All negative variables that can affect performance should be considered. Ensure that your team knows that you are available to listen to any concern or need that may be present. In order to build a strong relationship the simple fact is there are many intangibles involved in the process.

The main point that should naturally cultivate within the team is that success can be achieved if everyone ensures that the welfare for one another is always considered.

Honor

Leaders who challenge their teams to perform consistently at a high level, treat each team member with respect, dedicate time to develop the employee, value employee input, appreciate and recognize work efforts, most certainly will increase each individual's self esteem, character and gratification towards the business they serve.

The team's reputation for continuous achievement only strengthens each individual's opinion of the leader and the operation. The leader's straight forwardness and disciplinary practices will cultivate and enlighten the team to want to perform more as a collective unit until they instinctively comply with direction and accept new challenges with a sense of veracity and enthusiasm.

The leader drives the team's level of loyalty and commitment to the cause because it is the approach taken by that leader that will determine if the team exhibits honor or better yet the mark of distinction it decides to represent.

15

Evaluating Employee Work Performance

Is Project Red Light a tool for measuring employee work performance? There are major aspects of an individual's performance that can be determined based on how they performed within the program. It was mentioned in the introductory meeting that team contribution and effort was the central denominator in which each team member's performance will be evaluated. Some of the relevant behaviors that can be used for evaluation purposes are:

- Timely submission of Red Light forms

- Preparation for weekly meeting

- Technical development

- Teaming

- Contribution

- Communication

- Presentation skill development

- Analysis

- Mistakes learned vs. contribution made

- Flexibility

- Process feedback

- Completion of Red Light assignments

- Customer satisfaction achieved

- Issue escalation

- Team success

While individual development is achieved by incorporating the Project Red Light Program, it is the success of the collective body that is the central core of the improvement program. All individuals who played a role in team achievements should be given the appropriate praise for their performance.

Strategies

The following are some valuable tips on developing ideas and positioning recommendations throughout the program.

- Recommend multiple improvement ideas at one time to expose and mitigate the effectiveness of those in the decision-making process that dislike change and whose main objective is to thwart or delay the plan.

- Position low impact ideas around the main idea or most desired aspect of your improvement recommendation. Low impact ideas offer less benefit results.

- Know that some of the low impact ideas will be discarded after close examination and debate. This is alright. Your strategy is to allow these low impact ideas to be sacrificed as long as you gain approval for the main idea recommended. By doing so you have gained the advantage in the process and are positioned with a higher probability to gaining the appropriate approval desired.

- Be careful not to attach ideas that have no merit at all. This will not serve any purpose whatsoever. All ideas recommended should have supporting data that drive the recommendation.

- Always provide empowerment opportunities to team members. Provide situations where members have the opportunity to gain credibility within their team, their leadership and customers serviced. Make sure they know that you trust their judgment and that they have your approval to make sound decisions when confronted with urgent issues.

- Expect some decisions that do not result in a favorable outcome to occur. This is part of the learning process. Correct the situation. Explain what the appropriate response should have been. Ensure that you commend the individual for making decision. This will strengthen the relationship.

- Be realistic. Not all your business improvement ideas will be approved. Feeling a little failure keeps a leader humble. Pick up your head because tomorrow is another day.

- Gain approval for a pilot test. Keep the pilot as short as possible. Your intention is to gain credibility behind the solution and then provide tangible results. If someone states that we need a longer period to evaluate the results. Do your homework beforehand. Be prepared to provide a projected loss for extending the pilot.

- Be assertive and develop project improvement ideas quickly and effectively through the decision-making process. Customer needs are constantly changing and your ideas must change along with them. The worse mistake one can make is to initiate a lengthy project where ideas lose their excitement, support and potential benefits.

- Develop a mental toughness necessary to offset negative variables that will cross your path. Believe in yourself and your abilities to overcome any obstacles.

- Remember that one set of circumstances sets the stage for another set of circumstances. You decide the path to be taken. Be accountable for mistakes but share any successes equally with the rest of the team.

- Catalog the team's ideas generated. Many of those forgotten ideas may be resurrected based on a set of circumstances that you might experience in the future.

16

Beginning Your Project Red Light Journey; a Final Note to the Leader

Project Red Light has laid the road map for making continuous improvement a way of life for any team. You have been equipped with the knowledge, steps and tools necessary to naturally transform your workforce into a high performance team. The key component to begin the journey is to gain trust and establish a common desire from all who want to be the best.

As discussed throughout this book, the initiative begins when the collective unit establishes criteria that focus on the team's responsibility in meeting and exceeding customer satisfaction on a daily basis. A simple rating system brings to the forefront a multitude of service experiences which offer endless improvement opportunities.

Your employees will view their role in a different perspective once they are afforded the opportunity to take part in and make a significant contribution to the improvement process. Employee development will occur as project improvement fundamentals are learned. Lastly, the employee relationship will strengthen as collaboration, partnering and teaming occur. The empowering atmosphere you create will offer employees a true sense of ownership of the business results achieved.

The positives associated with Project Red Light are endless if you as the leader make the commitment to develop your employees. Offer opportunities to contribute to a common cause, and allow them to voice their opinions during the decision-making process. Your strong sense of commitment will be solidified as each individual realizes their potential. This is a catalyst to improve team morale and unity. You will be able to leverage resources to work on more challenging projects that in the past you found little time to complete. The potential benefits to any business will be significant.

This by no means is an easy undertaking. Coaching employees and empowering them to take ownership requires sacrifice and time on your part as the leader. A good leader takes the time to build a good team by coaching, teaching, facilitating, and changing behaviors. The improvement process is continuous and the journey is never ending.

As the leader the accountability for success or failure falls squarely on your shoulders. If you embrace this responsibility, you will reap the many benefits that will come along the way. I am certain that if the steps outlined in Project Red Light are followed, you will achieve the ultimate goal to improve the service experience for all involved—the *leader*, the *employee* and the *customer*.

Good luck on your journey.

0-595-33056-8